Thoughts
OF A
Soldier's Heart

Thoughts
OF A
Soldier's Heart

Quince R. Brown Sr.

Library of Congress Control Number: 2022907169

PAPERBACK: 978-1-957575-56-8
EBOOK: 978-1-957575-57-5

Ordering Information:

For orders and inquiries, please contact:
1-888-404-1388
www.goldtouchpress.com
book.orders@goldtouchpress.com

Printed in the United States of America

Contents

Acknowledgments

First and foremost I would like to thank my Lord and Savior Jesus Christ for bringing me this far in my life and sprinkling me with just a little bit of talent. If not for his grace and mercy I certainly would not have gotten here on my own. I would like to give thanks to my dear friend and motivator Edith Davis (R.I.P.).

Edith opened up in me a new meaning and understanding for writing in 1991 and once she got me started I was unable to look back. Edith passed away at too young an age and she is missed greatly by her children, her friends in the Public Affairs offices in the United States Army and most definitely by me.

I would like to thank my parents, sibling, and friends for being the sounding board for me on many occasions when I needed someone to hear my words. Their support and honesty over the years let me know if I felt what I wrote or wrote what I felt. I am honored to have such a wonderful family who continued to push me every time I felt like stopping.

In saving the best for last, I would like to thank my wife Jennifer. She is my Wife, my Queen and my Love. I have written more in the last three years that I had written in the previous ten. She draws out the very best in me and I appreciate that. It seems at times I can look upon her and within minutes the words fall upon me. She has been my biggest supporter during the final makings of this book and if not for her I may still have everything in a file draw gathering dust. Thanks a bunch my sweetie, I Love you.

Sir Ladric Hylton BKA Quince R. Brown Sr.
May 2015

To my Grandfather,

Ladrick Joseph Nathaniel Hylton

Although I had never physically seen or known him,
I believe his spirit has always lived in me and kept me.
I Love you Papa.

A Parent's Tears

Today I am one year old and it is supposed to be the happiest day of the year
There's cake and lots of toys, plenty of ice cream for baby girls and boys
And yet when I look at my mother her eyes look to me like they are filled
    with tears.
I turned four just the other day - going to school would soon be under way
Hurry daddy please get me to the school gate its my first day I just cannot
    be late
When I get to class and wave goodbye its seemed like my daddy had tears
    in his eyes
Ah, junior high has now approached and yet the thing I fear the most
Is leaving all of those I had made friends - during preschool right to my
    grade school's end
I'm getting older now just hit my teens - although I don't know what it
    really means
I've heard in time I'll really see —teen responsibilities can be extreme
My parents watch me gallop through junior high with smiles and big tears
    in their eyes
High school I'm sixteen and I am almost grown - at least my friends all
    tell me so
I eat, drink or sleep only when I want - time to make decisions on my own
This time of life I have no fear - yet my parents still seem to be shedding
    tears
Graduation day now I am so free - no school no parents no responsibilities -
    just me
I am my own person I let it be known - I am ready for the world I can whip
    the unknown

Then reality hits and I now have bills, insurance, groceries and rent - I am
    not prepared
Life is not that easy I am now aware I begin to think back on my parents
    tears
I have put off college it will have to wait - my hormones are raging so I
    begin to date
I'm going steady now and soon find out - we are to be parents without a
    doubt
Now my friend and I have both become scared — and we have now begun
    to shed our tears
I work all day and part of the night - doctor bills and frustration my friend
    and I fight
If this is what parenting will be all about - I should have gone to college
    and never gotten out
For this part of life I was not prepared - little by little I began to understand
    all the tears
My daughter was born just yesterday - the night before I knelt bowed my
    head and prayed
Asking GOD for help of the days ahead - with her first step, first school
    and first cut as she bled
I Prayed for patience when she misunderstood - I prayed for guidance to
    teach her good
I Prayed for knowledge to help make her smart - I prayed for love to fill
    her tiny heart
Most of all I prayed that I may be wise - so I can one day help her realize
That what she sees are drops of Love not tears - she may sometimes see in
    her parents eyes.

Baby It's Cold Outside

Baby it's cold outside
Was the text in December that Jennifer sent
Words spoken through unchattering teeth
So I stopped to ponder what she meant
And I am sure the poise she showed
Was glamorous and caused her skin to glow
A hint of caramel and glimmer of pecan
Just a pinch of almond mystifying any man
A little brown sugar and a cinnamon stick
Those lips and hips hypnotize me quick
And although outside may have a chill
The flame from her heart warms my heart still
When I try my best not to advance
Still I am unable to escape her eyes
The cold that she speaks of outside
Is only for the ears of a man that's wise
One who can embrace the warmth of her arms
Or is lucky to touch her fingers at best
Let alone put his head on her shoulder
Or snuggle his face to the fold of her breasts
Still I remember last summer I heard those words
Yet before its true meaning would hide
Now I know when she wants me to share her love
She says "Baby its cold outside"

Baby Talk

Will you stay for a while till I've grown
Are you here to make our house a home
Can you stick around till I become and adult in age
Will you come see my play, watch me on stage
Can you attend some of my sporting events
And follow me whenever and wherever I went
Maybe take a day off to push me on a swing
Or sit and drink tea as I played with my things
Can you write me a song and maybe I can sing
Just tell me what to do and how to begin
How do you feel I should start off my day
And what are the things you want to hear me say
Teach me in life all that I should do
And what to say when people ask what I call you
How long will I be able to count our days
And do you want to be permanent here or just another phase
I promise I will work hard in school to get an "A"
If you punish me in the house I promise I'll stay
If when you're done you hug me you can spank me any day
As long as you let me watch you grow old and get gray
I don't know if I can keep you and yet
In my heart I believe you're as good as it gets
Are you here to make our house a home
Will you stay for a while till I've grown
Do you hear me Daddy?

Brainmatters

Am I Wise, Intelligent or even smart
I speak words with meaning but they seem to lack heart
Do I convey with emotions things causing commotions?
Is the picture I paint a comic, illustration or devotion
Do my words create dollars or make sense
Will my increase be with others or simply solidarity
Are my philosophies intense a glancing blow or pretense?
Am I interested in true results or popularity?
I need a friend more than I need an ear
I see the bright lights through the eyes of a panicking deer
My words and your mind must come together as a pair
Because you can't see what I say lest it appear
E= MC square ok this is true
Two is a duo so now I do what is due
I come to you to help with my problems
When I'm angry I can't see well or be well enough to solve them
Solvent, something to keep my knees bent when I vent
Evolvement of Involvement does it mean what I meant
Life spent I Hyperventilate do you understand
My words being banned is not the plan that I planned
And still I am going through all this hell I can't quell
This has to be a spell not just a hole where I fell
So I reach up with my hand that's not broken
You said that would be here if the words "I Need You" were spoken
My pride has been revoked my spirit is now broken
I barely breathe and my own words that I speak leave me chocking
What I experience is pain cursing through all of my veins
I can't explain won't complain so long as I don't go insane
For in order to have peace and maintain
My Matters only matters if matters of my brain

Can I

The other day while walking I stopped and thought
How good you looked in the scarf I bought
And admired your nice fit in your blouse and your skirt
If it's ok Can you and I flirt
Can I reach out and hold your hand and pretend that I could be your man
And take a stand at your right side then open my chest so my heart can't hide
Or duck away to a silent place or take fleet of foot as its beats race
Or cover itself in the darkest hole or disappear to the world like a mole
Can I caress your arms and legs and back and protect you from all of life's
    attacks
Or black every man's vision who may be inclined to prevent you from being mine
Can I bring you flowers on any given day whether sunny, rainy or clouds at play
Or run you some water to give you a bath and picture our futures path
Can I brush your hair and rub your skin when you give me that innocent grin
Or steady you before you fall if you would allow me to give you my all
Can I for you go gather the stars or buy you a house or boat or a car
If you want I will reset the moon to make sure it's light is never too far
Can I spend time in your space or even give you the key to my place
To make sure each morning I woke I would embrace your beautiful face
Can I take you to church with me so you could know the GOD I see
And thank him time and again because he has blessed my soul with thee
Can I share my favorite book and song so our nights will always last long
Or maybe study our bible together to keep our beliefs going strong
Can I take you into my life I think growing old with you would be nice
I will love, honor and respect you I only ask that you be my wife
CAN I Sweetie, CAN I

Chance

I hoped by chance to beg a dance
    and hold you near so you could feel
how loud you cause my heart to beat
    or feel the dampness of my palms
and see the sparkles in my eyes
    and watch the way I glow to know
that on this eve you'll be my prize
    By chance I'd stroll across the floor
reach for your hand and then demand
    you give me dance and then by chance
this night should end in true romance
    and as you turned to me I thought
how can it be I am so blessed
    that God would send an angel which
I would hold close against my chest
    And so by chance the dance began
one that I hoped would last my life
    a hug that started out as friends
I hoped would end as husband and wife
    now all my dreams, my wish, desires
has come so real this I do feel
    but only for when I did glance
by chance you granted me a dance

Change Me

I want to be a better person than whom I am
I want to give you all that I can
I want to make you as happy as can be
So I want you to help me change me
I don't want to wake up alone in my home
I don't want to be forgotten with each age I grow
I want to smell roses and travel across seas
I want you to help me change me
I'd like the opportunity to take a vacation
Or ride a motorcycle across this great nation
I want to interact I don't just want to see
I want you to help me change me
I want to be with you each and every day
I'd like to watch as our grandchildren play
I want to hold your hand as you sit beside me
I want you to help me change me
I want to enjoy clouds when no suns in sight
Or take a long walk on starless nights
And express to you how you fill me with glee
I want you to help me change me
I want have dances with you in the rain
Then go in get dry and get wet again
I want our lips to have a kissing spree
I want you to help me change me
I want you to show me all kinds of stuff

I want you to make sure I read my bible enough
I want we are able to agree to disagree
I want you to help me change me
I so long to learn what love is about
I wish to converse without one yell or shout
I'd like for my heart to be one with thee
I want you to help me change me
When my days have passed and I lay to rest
And I stand before God for my final test
I hope the Pearly Gates will grant entry
So I may thank you for helping me change me

Dance In Our Sleep

Fallen nights the sun has gone down
Cricket whistles and darkness fills the town
I put on my suit and you slide in your gown
Heads pressed side by side my arms open wide
You press close slide your body inside
You to me and I to you we confide
In each other our hands do clasp
With one another we match with class
Our feet prepare to begin the event
This grand occasion for us was meant
Our knees ever so slightly they touch
My midsections blush as you nestle your butt
Tight up against me I truly enjoy we
This seems a collage and I am unable to see me
This is no mirage what my heart sees is thee
As the hours pass us by
You will turn and I shall spin
You move out and I within
You press back and I push on
Until the night is finally gone
Day break you shimmy I shake And then we wake
We smile and speak not a single peep
Only our hearts have tired from exhaustion
Because we Dance in our Sleep

Death's Life

In my life
I have wished and plead
I have mourned and begged
I have cursed and raged
I have fought I have slain
I have screamed and cried
I have stolen also lied
I have slandered I have hurt
I have made my bed in dirt

In my life
I have gone and came
I have punished and maimed
I have damaged I have scared
I have left many faces marred
I have ridiculed and spat
I have labeled many this and that
I have cheated I have vandalized
and then I finally realized
I never existed in this life I despised
for at birth I had already died.

You Were There

Remember the other day when you asked me for a minute
To listen to an issue and maybe help you with it
And I stated not at the time, because I had things on my mind
My work was way behind and I had some stuff I had to find -
    So you walked away
Remember the other night when you called my phone
And asked if I had time and could stop by your home —
And I said not today, because I had to go get my car out the shop
Then get that gospel CD that was about to drop - **So you said ok**
Remember the other morning when you said you needed to talk
And I told you sure but you had to do it while we walked
Because I had to do a greeting and ensure the proper seating
For some very important people that were coming to my meeting -
    So you said another time
Remember that night that you sent me a text
And said you were in a bind and did not know what to do next
And I said we would talk after I got some rest
Because I had presentation in the morning and I wanted to do my best -
    So you said never mind
Remember that time a loved one passed away
You called and told me you really needed me that day
And I said I wished I could and hoped you understood
But I was beat for the party last night and did not feel too good -
    So you said that's fine

Hey you are my friend and I want to be there its true
But how many times were you there for me like you want me there for you
Let me think
What about when I lost my wallet and had no money — you were there
What about the day when I was sick and felt funny — you were there
What about that time I was short and had to pay my rent — you were
    there
What about my birthdays, promotions or my special events — you
    were there
What about the time I crashed my car into the pole — you were there
What about the months I was depressed and slipped into a hole — you
    were there
What about the day that my baby was born — you were there
And even the night daddy went to sleep and the Lord took him home —
    you were there
WOW - Remembering those things makes me realize how good you
    have been
I wish I saw in you whatever in me that you have seen
Now I understand throughout these years with you I am Blessed
And when people speak of being a brother's keeper
I will them that YOU are the best.
Thank you Lord for Always being there.

Demons

In all ways the Demons are smarter than I.
I am wisdomless in comparison as they are
wittier and keener than I.
They are craftier
than I could ever imagine to be.
I need to
but cannot fight this fight.
What allows a man
to want to fight a fight
he is bound to lose.

The Chase

The CHASE has again begun and the games are on.
In exhaustion I continue to move.
Wearily and unable to breathe still I move.
Am I running from or running to?
What chases me but me?
Am I even running at all?
I am so tired and beaten.
My joints hurt, my muscles cramp and my lungs burn.
I am afraid to keep running and yet more afraid to stop.
So what is left?
Stop this un-winning game Lord.
Stop this game I pray

My Valentine

Baby you are forever <u>My Valentine</u>

I see you blushing more than the reddest of wine

The heart I felt beating is yours not mine

And the vision I see of you is fine, fine, fine

It soothes me to sit and speak with you a while

And that hat you wear sure shows off your style

Could you tilt your head a little so I can enjoy your smile

For you a brother would bunny hop a country mile

You know I like that dress that flares when you twirl

I can think of no other that leaves my heart so unfurled

I have more joy than a oyster with a ten pound pearl

Cause in my heart I know that you are my girl

Since you're able to make my heart flutter and rise

I now ask for help to make my mind wise

With you my love has been put to the test

And I need to make sure I stay blessed

Why is it when you're happy you often like to clap

Whenever you're irritated I get a finger snap

When I try to explain something you just roll those eyes

And if I prove I'm right you twist your head to the side

When I hold you close you do a shoulder shimmer

If I'm late and did not call I get a "Psssst did you say dinner"

You knew when we met I was a man thus a sinner

But give me credit, I made sure one of us picked a winner

From your head to your toe there is one thing I know

You and I are twisted, wrapped up and entwined

And with every passing day — I'll proclaim, pray and say

Boo you are forever <u>My Valentine</u>

Sleep

Morning breaks
Cool air and brisk wind
My breath it takes
Without care draws it from within
Eyes overglossed red
Lack of oxygen
And a groggy head
Foggy thoughts
Leaving me misled
My sleep for naught
Actually, did I ever go to bed?

Indeed

Hands on the clock, tick no tock
Boat on the waters sail no dock
Strong waves so we rock
And roll, the toll it takes
The fret it makes our minds irate
Patience I have yet still can't wait
Temptation, we take the bait and bite
No quarrels no fight but fright
With delight we invite angry feelings
Stacked decks makes for bad dealings
Wounds knee deep need healings
Skin tattered and torn scab peeling
Pulled off tossed out make sure no doubts but don't shout
Speak calm, soothing ointment, healing balm
We rub slow, scars stay but we desire they go
Running fast yet moving slow, I know, we grow
Weight of my sins I drag in tow, oh
I owe, but what I sow only GOD will know
Grab on, though here almost gone so far
100 miles an hour on foot no car
Lying in my street gunshots no war
Twinkling autumn nights and yet no star
Imprisoned locked in my mind but no bars
Facts stated, I infuriated, we debated, you placated
We wait passing nights, so dark soon dawn
I follow, lead on, I swallow you feed
Not hunger just greed we bite the hands they bleed
I appeal then peel away fake so we see what's real
I want I take I won't steal - I pray for breaks then I kneel
I give my spiel truth makes me heal his words I'll heed - Indeed

Protector

If I don't hold my loved ones close in my arms
Keep them calm or sing them a Psalm
Wipe the tears, erase the fears that appear
Always try to be there or at least near
That I can hear when they call
Catch them if they fall or
Give them a hand over the tall wall
Help them continue should they stall
Be understanding and never act appalled
No matter the situation
Just give realization
That there will come a day of confrontation
And if not temporary evasion
The end result will cause devastation
Digging deep to the soul
That the frustration will over take
And inflate the growing power of hate
That cannot be escaped
But causes a debate enough to incarcerate
The heart and unable to elude the true fact
That I must protect my loved ones
From Satans unyielding attacks
No matter the consequence I have their back

Faith

Childless, dealt life's ill fate, in secluded state she lay in wait
pondering   her   own   death   now   for   a   while
will   it   capture   her   as   it   did   her   child
forty   years   in   age   and   some   days   more
her   hopes   for   a   child   seems   a   losing   war
"you   have   been   cursed"
her   friends   all   cry
7   and   20   months
a   third   stillborn   child
more   shocking   news   from   her   doctors   indeed
she   could   never   survive   another   pregnancy
no medicines of this world, could fill her womb with a boy or girl
a heavy tear, undying pride, bent knees bowed head a subtle sigh,
folded hands, a loving smile, she says
"Thank   you   Lord
for   my   future   child"
years have   passed,   exactly   five,
still she   prays   still she   smiles,
her spirit glows and when asked why
"for God has blessed me" she replies
others   ask   is   she   not   scared
"no" she says   "I've found prayer"
for nine months   all   anticipate
a girl is born appropriately named
F   A   I   T   H
all asked in prayer if one believes
when   you   ask   the   Lord
you   shall   receive

Mystery

The mystery is not as I thought it to be
It has come clear for me to see - and yet
I now realize it is something I cannot get
Happiness eludes me as I elude myself
Again trying to outsmart my own heart
Ducking the corner and closing the door
Turning off the lights lying on the floor
Praying that not even GOD sees my shame
I keep telling myself that I can win this game
My mind has become black
From the internal attacks
Again I feel I am falling off track
No longer blind to the fact
I cannot find my way back
Is it for lack of effort
That I keep coming up short
I sometimes wish my mother had me abort-ted
This way I could have been born dead
But instead

I have to live through this life
Headaches, pain, suffering and strife
Trying to stay married and hold on to my wife
And be a better father to my kids
Put my hands over my ears
And pray the steam does not blow my lid
Or whistle out in the dark when I hid
My clothes soak wet from the cold sweats
My head spinning from lack of breath
This is the road I had hoped not to travel
For now I trod through the valley of death
Lord I pray to you to pull me through
Lift me up so at your table I can sup
Hold my hand guide a spiritually blind man
Hear my screams and read my dreams
I hope surely you've heard what I said
For at this time in my life I am in no hurry
To take up residence the land of the dead

Strange

Strange it seems
how you perceive
that all my needs are out of greed
but yet you flaunt the wants that you've received
are all necessities
      Strange that is
      if I do wrong
      you're quick to leave me all alone
      yet burden me by every means
      to mend your wounds and stop your bleeds
            Strange in how
            I'd give my shirt
            to shield your heart from dirt and hurt
            yet even still you'd steal my soul and hopes
            of all my future's goals
                  Strange you say
                  because I show you care
                  for all my every days
                  and yet I know for sure
                  you have no love for me in any way

And though I know for me you've never cared or ever would be true
and with each passing day you'll only leave me feeling less than blue
and though I know you tell me lies as you stare in my saddened eyes
STRANGE it seems I cannot fight the fact I'm still in love with you

Journey

Are you ready to take this journey with me
To see sights together to a place unknown
Where not even grass has grown, or land has been owned
To step down on the ground and be bound by the vines of passion
The initial reaction is to scream or panic, heart thumping be frantic
Trying to escape what is actually the calm and the palm of my hand
Rest you head on the shoulder of this man if you can
Or dare to take part in this affair - ok just stop — now stare
Into the eyes of your prize
Should you decide to claim me, tame me brand and name me
Call me your own, let it be known
By you I am now possessed no — repossessed, stripped naked, undressed
Bathe me in your, tears, fears, worries and cares
Allow me to extend my arms, your woes I'll calm your heart I'll warm
With whispered words from my lips your mouth touches mine
You sip my emotions my bodily wine
Your head now spins your mind inclined to be seduced
You have no clue, but do, to me, wish to be true
And given the chance you beg for enhanced romance
Despite the possibility of pain, you want, you need
To lay in my rain again
While trying to maintain you logic
Still your tongue with mine wish to frolic
As playful swords who adore the chore of penetration
In overdrive is your imagination, step to me such adoration
Let us crawl, walk and run as long as we succumb
To the WE - I am no good alone as you can see
Let me be your <u>W</u> and you my <u>E</u>
Are you ready to take this journey with me

Recovery

Remember when I arrived many days ago

Everyday seemed a fight in my soul

Counselors saying when where and why

Only want to get through but not try

Vested now in a reason I must confess

Every day I work harder I feel blessed

Rather than give up I'll give my best

Yes recovery is the means to my success

To Wish To Pray

I wish so much to have you near
    to hold you close within arms reach
        to free your mind from thoughts of fear
            allowing love to just appear
                and give your soul a little peace
I wish for just a given chance
    to show my care and prove my worth
        let our love be our future's birth
            for knew I did upon first glance
                you alone, makes my heart dance
                    and truly if it is you I crave
                then trust I can't in just a wish
            for knowing <u>GOD</u> hears thoughts I say
to have you I know I must Pray

Forgotten We

I stand in the prison gates and before me all I see
The faces of men of different color, creed, races and nationality
All with different desires ideas imagination and needs
Different thoughts in their head but when cut the color red they bleed
The more I look and saw and thought I thought I saw the look they fought
The more I opened up my eyes the more inside I realized
All I actually see is the reflection of he who I call me
I see they need help in their life, I see the demons who share their nights
I see they just know black or white they get what's left you take what's right
They live my life to their delight Its done in spite of plight or pain
Crazed membrane entertains insane confused migraine and thick veined
*   brain*
Thought what thought not how soon it is you forgot they're not just spots
There is no difference between us except the fact that they got caught
Give me a shirt, let me go in with them within a week I'll blend
Confess the things I done back then, speak of my bad, my shame my sin
Although I did not call it that on my head it sat under my hat
So no one saw, my flaw, my awe, my disregard for my GOD's law
I know once inside I'll be forget, gates lock, days run together no clock
Decision I made, anger afflicted, jury convicted, punishment inflicted
Now here stripped clean shaven bald no care no hair no fear just despair
What I did wrong - whatever it was on that day that you thought you seen
You don't know me how can you see my deeds, what I believe, or my creed
What I fight for, my battle scars my wars are not behind these bars
My instruction, no discussion head concussion mass destruction
I am nobody I cannot be seen, not by your eye, not past your beam
My I in my team, my thoughts my dream, my vision my life seem so serene
My thought to the world - take no plea, no bargains no plans of things to be
So lets disagree to agree that you do you
For you've already FORGOTTEN about WE

The Chase 2

Why must the CHASE be so harsh?
Why can't the demons let me be?
I cannot seem to turn the right corner
or find the right door to hide behind.
I want to scrape the sores off my feet
dig my flesh from my bones.
If I have no flesh it cannot be weak.
I need not submit to that which weakens me.
Pluck my eyes from their sockets.
If I cannot see I cannot be tempted.
What do I need to do Lord to fall into your good graces?
My heart burns like molten rocks
my mind is confused for the sake of confusion.
Lord do you hear me?
My GOD, do I hear myself?

Peace

The peace grows
The anger fights to get out
But as a vine the peace grows
My ribs, kidneys, liver, lungs all hurt
From the fight within
The peace grows
The crying is senseless
As it neither helps or hurts
It is wasted effort
The peace grows
I must learn to grow with the peace
Not get caught behind
Stuck on the roots
I must move with the vine
The peace grows

That Black Dress

I can envision her in that beautiful black dress
Strolling across the floor and I must confess
That eyes are glued
To her hips as they move, as they sway with a groove
The stares all prove while the mouths say whoooh
When she finally takes her seat
One knee crossed over the other thigh
That black dress not too low yet just so high
Smooth legs not a single hair can be seen
Pretty face gorgeous feet and so damn sexy inbetween
One heck of a menu
That any man can freely view
But cannot order any food unless his name is Q
That black dress
That shimmies when she stands
Shakes when she extends her hand
And totally distorts thoughts of the above average man
That black dress
Showing off the strength of her shoulders
Yet can hold and caress
The tight waist and fullness of her natural breasts
That black dress
That is accentuated by her heels
That when she turns it reveals
What is the true meaning of sex appeal
That what will make a man kneel
Crawl, beg and even plead
For her address and a chance to undress
That stunningly sexy woman in that Damn Black Dress

Memories Of We

Let them take my sense of sight I need it not to see
 the beauty that you seem to hold so deep inside of thee
Let them take my sense of sound I need it not to hear
 your laughs, cries, joys and pains which initially drew me near
Let them take my sense of smell I need it not to know
 that only your sweet fragrance can stir my very soul
Let them take my sense of taste to keep it only make me miss
 the soft and honey coated lips with each departing kiss
Let them take my sense of touch I need it not to feel
 the warmth we shared with each embrace which left me so unreeled
And when they think I'm beaten and they've taken it all away
 and left me here with little hope of living another day
I'd even let them take my life and still it could not take from me
 that which I store deep in my heart my Memories of We

Resembles Me

I STARE AT THE SWIRLING PUDDLE
AND IT SEEMS I SEE
A HE WHO RESEMBLES ME
AND YET HIS BROW IS FROWNED
HIS LIPS THEY BOW
TURN UPSIDE DOWN
BLANK PUPILS BLACK
REVERSED IN DIRECTION
THEY LOOK BACK
YET MAKE NO CONNECTION
NO THOUGHT NO RECOLLECTION
NO IDEA NO DIRECTION
THEY NOW SHOW FEAR
HAVE NO PROTECTION
EYES WEEP HALF SHUT
THEY PEEP NOW WHAT
HE WHO MIRRORS ME
IS TRYING HIS BEST
IT SEEMS TO FLEE
AND AS I STARE
AT THE PUDDLE'S SWIRL
I STILL SEE HE
WHO RESEMBLES ME

Of Twisted Minds

Of twisted minds — I don't mind
Is there realization of annihilation
of our very civilization
Are we stuck in place - adolescence
and lack of maturation
A perplexed thought
Desires to excel and succeed all for naught
Have we sold our souls to the highest bidder
To have reign over all
including the rain
Are we to indulge
in the bulge of our expanding pockets
In order to buy love or do we call her Venus
Is it our hearts that swells or our penis
The growth of sensation
Thought of penetration
Yet our imaginative concentration
Leaves us empty
Spilling our seed on our bed
M A S T E R B A T I O N
Relief - - Belief - - Grief
O yeah - I remember now
I don't mind - The twisted mind

HIDING FROM MYSELF

When I look to the mirror I see no reflection there
    no image comes to greet me whether I should peep or stare
my heart and brain still operate I know that I still live
    and yet I cannot see me, no reflection does my mirror give
yet if another passerby does cross that mirrors view
    I'm quick to see their ugliness and faults they may do
because the life I live does daily jeopardize my health
    this I think be reason why I'm Hiding from Myself
Untruthfulness, a milder term of what one calls a lie
    but guilty I am not unless you see me with my eyes
I can't escape the witnessing of my own horrid sins
    so I just call them secrets and keep them locked within
I ponder why my life sometimes may suddenly stand still
    can it be that my evils makes my dreams all unfulfilled
until I come to realize my soul's ice I must melt
    a victory is unreachable while Hiding from Myself

My First Love

She was in her 20's when I first saw her face
A vision of loveliness, intelligence and grace
I realized if beauty would determine a victor she was sure
to win the race
Her arms were soft and smooth and brown her hair black
as a ravens wing
I remember she held me so close that even now I smell her
sweetened skin
Lavender, cocoa, almonds and honey scents I recognized
as she drew me near
I'd shut my eyes and then open them again always hoping
she still was there
I had found in this woman a friendship that has lasted
over the years
I had shared with this woman my deepest thoughts,
doubts, worries and fears
I have laughed with this woman many days until my eyes
had filled with tears
I have trusted this woman with my life because for me this
woman always cared
On many a day when it seemed that confusion was all I knew
I would call on this woman as she was always there to get
me through
Regardless if I was in her presence or very far away
She still knew how to soothe my heart and exactly what
to say
I know many times we often think no one can read our mind
I realized it was possible for this special woman of mine
There have been some times in my life that to her I was not
true

There have been some days I caused her pain by not doing
what I should do
There have been some questions in my distant past I did
not answer true
And still she continued to love me though these things she
already knew
I am not quite sure what she sees in me not sure why she
believes in me
not sure why for me she stays but I'm sure every day for
me she prays
I have judged and compared other women to the standard
she has set
I have probably subconsciously left a few if her standards
were not met
I have given compliments time again and always tried to
be fair
But there are very few women I have known whose legs
were a prettier pair
No matter how much she has seen me cry no matter how
often she dried my eyes
No matter if my days seem like nights she was always able
to make me feel right
This if for my special woman and first love I knew in my life
The only woman I could possibly love more than a wife
GOD has replaced her as my first love now and to her it is
no bother
Because a part of my heart still belongs to Lynnette, the
first Love I knew was
MY MOTHER

That's My Dad

He works Monday to Sunday all year long
    his body may weaken but heart stays strong
        in order to provide us what he never had
            him, that guy, oh   "THAT'S MY DAD"
He barely has time to drink the tea in his cup
    still he strives on never desiring to give up
        his emotions maintained so as not to get mad
            him, that guy, oh   "THAT'S MY DAD"
If the car breaks down he rides the bus
    should the bus get a flat he still doesn't fuss
        his spirit stays happy though his eyes look sad
            him, that guy, oh   "THAT'S MY DAD"
He's missed some of my functions and that's OK
    see we never missed meals cause he worked and got paid
        "He is one great cook" hearing that makes me glad
            him, that guy, oh   "THAT'S MY DAD"
His plaid pants he wore still makes me smile
    I suppose he thought he was really in style
        thank GOD it was only a passing fad
            yeah the old man, oh   "THAT'S MY DAD"
He is admirable and indeed a hard working man
    when he makes up his mind he sticks to the plan
        he will always push forward regardless of hurt
            for his children he'd go naked and give his last shirt
        always fighting the battle no succumbing to pain
    he has nothing to lose the whole world to gain
he's one of the best friend's that I've ever had
        That guy "CHARLIE B", oh "THAT'S MY DAD"

Mr. Clown

His shoes are big his nose so red
he laughs and shouts and bops his head
outside he seems so full of glee
inside he's dead from toe to head
> Mr. Clown's painted face of blues and greens
> can fill all hearts with hopes and dreams
> but wipe it clean and you will meet
> a look of grief and pure defeat

Day in day out the fans all shout
bring out Mr. Clown and make us laugh
he falls as he runs for everyone's fun
but be thankful you've never run his path
> Oh yes Mr. Clown just loves the days
> when all the crowd applauds his play
> though when the lights go out at night
> throughout his mind the demons play

Mr. Clown lives His life to entertain
to ease discomfort to stop your pains
yet deep inside his hurts he hides
to ensure he makes you laugh again
> When the day comes to close and everyone leaves
> when the spotlight does finally go down
> take a chance of a glance or a stare if you dare
> for there's tears in the eyes of Mr. Clown

Why

Why do my hands leave my mouth wide open yet cover my eyes

Why is it though I walk with destruction when it happens I act surprised

Why say what I really mean in my heart and then try to apologize

Why when I roll around in shit I don't expect to be followed by flies

Why when I know I am bound to fail why even bother to try

Why when I have been caught dead to rights my guilt I try to deny

Why are the words coming out my mouth actually still stuck in my head

Why does my voice sound good to me but seems to hurt others instead

Why is it that rage comes out my veins each time I bled

Why is it the thought of waking everyday is something I dread

Why when success knocks my front door out the back I fled

Why is the only time I don't cause pain is when I'm alone in bed

Why is it every relationship I get in I want to leave

Why is the person not really what I thought I had received

Why is it no matter what I try in me she cannot believe

Why is it when it ends in turmoil my spirit seems so relieved

Why do I block the path to freedom whenever someone tries to get by

Why do I always come up short — because myself I don't really apply

Why is it with all the knowledge I drink my brain still always feels dry

Why though tears streak down my face I will never admit that I cry

Why does my worst come out though there are good thoughts I imply

Why I ponder time and again — Why in hell ask **Why**

Shadow

As I move so it does also
As we stand upright so it does grow
As we suffer with pains so it does slow
In my feet and below I see it show

Whether sun or rain its there I know
Whether I walk or run its near and fro
Whether light as a feather I have it to tow
In my feet and below I see it show

If winter should arrive it lays on snow
If spring brings the grass it can lay below
If summer heat arrives in waves it flows
In my feet and below I see it show

So as I age and also grow slow
I know back and fro it I tow
In the snow or below still it flows
Let the world see it show

SEE MY SHADOW!!

The Chase 3

Now it is both shoulders I look over as I run.
The swelling in my feet increase and yet
not as fast as the growing welts on my back from the beatings.
Strapped to a wall and punished so that all can witness
Then go confess, about the mess I invited into my life
Handed the keys to the demons, lifted my arms so my ribs could welcome the knife
Still trying to run away from what I call strife.
Fingernailess, spots of blood spackle white sands I crawl through.
I fight the man with hands around my neck and foot in my chest
Now I realize the hands are mine yet the choking continues
Still I am unable to blackout with no desire to stay conscious.
I welcome the stinging stares, hated glares
Gut wrenching blows and blood that flows down my cheek from my eyes corner.
I thought them tears.
What I shed are the actual demons that grow and chase me.
It is me from whom I flee that I see.

Worst Enemy

My life as I live is my own
I go and come as I please
I enjoy all good things
that my life does bring
never rushing always living with ease
and yet it now seems
that all of my dreams
are slipping quite far from my reach
for so blind am I that I cannot see
that I am my worst enemy

There is much pleasure offered to me
by those who set me on high
a warm cheerful look
a laugh or a smile
or a hug so often desired
so one would believe
with all I've received
a life of a king I would lead
but my fate is a must
and I will self destruct
for I am my worst enemy.

I Need You

Tearful, salted water fill my eyes
I have come to realize and now emphasize
If I apply the feelings of my mind Search my soul's corner I may find
My not seeing before is not that I was blind or eyes were shut
I just forgot to lift the lids of my heart
Remove the blinders from my soul, Smother the cold
Create a flame, scream out your name
While we are intertwined, bodies combined
Sharing a stirred in mixed up melted down mind
Thoughts passing passionately
Tongue mashed against tongue
Till they look like one - member
This we will always remember
Through 50 years of Septembers
Or winters, summers and springs
You are my other being for being what my heart not my eyes are seeing
The beats that beat is slow and constant-ly
You I want, leave me don't, forget you I cant
Slow for a minute, you and I, us, we are infinite while intimate
In the moonlight we meet, we greet, we become carnal beasts
Bodies speak, on each other we feast to each other we are sweet
Us together cannot feel defeat with each other we are totally

complete Because - **I Need You**

A Prison – A Haven

Immersed in water from toe to head I breathe and yet I shall not drown
I'm protected from the land of dead whether rightside up or upside down
and even though the walls are close and I have no means of escape
I smile cause I choose not to leave life in here for me is great
The prison walls are very thin not made of brick or even steel
yet so strong it keeps me within my guardian and my daily shield
attached by some mysterious rope that feeds me although I don't eat
freedom is quite limited and yet I feel my life is so complete
Happy as I am my contentment fades,
greed seeks out a passage through
shunning the care I had received I'm inquisitive so this I must do
I see a light from a distance off an opening at my prisons floor
freedom indeed is what I thought a greater domain is through that door
So I swim on towards this gate head first full speed my only care
but once outside I gasp for air for I know now I'm truly scared
I receive a greeting of unpleasant style a blow I feel may break my bones
enough to make me realize how blessed I was in my solitary home
and as I look back to my exit way my warden gives only a halfway smile
for she knows had I known my escape be this world
I'd have stayed in my prison for a longer while.

This Day

Some days seem to be repeats of the previous days events
Things we say and wish we didn't as they were things we never meant —
Yet they spewed out our mouths based on feelings that we felt,
so then we vent let loose our belts to ensure the our victims would show the welts
Intentional, not intended for ALL who had to hear it
the blanket of evil tongues, unfortunately ALL now have to wear it,
Foul and filthy words burning our lungs as we exhale it
heat greater than the fire in the mouth of a dragon and that is no myth
We people are in a dilemma, a degradable position a bad situation
Not easily pulled out like and indentation not easily cured with medication
If we knew in advance the hurt we cause, I believe we would pause and
consider our flaws transform into wildcats and
produce our paws, fight for the cause, flash our claws and show the teeth of
the great white - JAWS.
Even after the flames are removed the fire still leaves a mark
how large the explosion how little the spark,
how huge the sea yet the pond so small
Only at the beginning does size ever matter at all.
Often it is not what we say but how we say it,
It is not the answers that are given but how the recipient portrays it
If we give up on all we should not and forgot
all that God had planned for us we would certainly have not
We cannot continue to live in fear or be scared
Yet we doubt our existence to be here or to care.
This day will be mine to conquer and defeat,

I will know I'll have won when the next 24 are complete, when sunshine is
the lights in the streets and when calm not bitter
anger are the words that I speak
I will avoid those ladies that try to get in my way,
Miss-interpretation, Miss-understanding and of course Miss-take
They try to twist every word that I say,
so I pray hoping God will speak for me if for him I obey,
When others hear my words as they are finally arranged,
I hope I am not deranged I hope they will not complain
This is the DAY that the Lord has made
I will rejoice and be glad as I call on Jesus name
I hope that when I die I leave as peaceful as I came
*and I am remembered for my character in how I tried to live **THIS DAY.***

Special Tribute To The Family Of
Edith Davis

PONDER THIS

If it is I that you desire

Come huddle with me close by the fire

To watch the flames flickering and knowing

Mirroring my heart of desires are growing

To a point somewhere beyond time or deed

Rushing through flashes of heat and need

As I lay wondering and amazed

Closed are my eyes and yet I gaze

As cosmic visions racing clearly by

Our mind eternal our hearts do fly

Swiftly above a spectral haunting

Of our two souls longing and wanting

Free-writing by Quince R. Brown Sr & Edith Davis April 1991

TRIBUTE TO MY LORD AND SAVIOR JESUS CHRIST

Christ Lives

UNtested	Courage
UNtouched	Heart
UNcontrolled	Rage
Unused	Intelligence
UNecessary	Sadness
UNknown	Trust
UNconditional	Love
UNfelt	Importance
UNavailable	Victory
Unseen	Emotions
UNsaved	Soul

UNtil JESUS

Sir Ladric Hylton